Contents

Preface

There are certain basic principles which we, as practising teachers, have come to value. This book has been written in the hope that it will help Key Stage 1 teachers who share those beliefs to implement them in their own practice.

The book gives a variety of ideas and is intended for both the specialist and non-specialist. There are a number of ways teachers could use the ideas. Firstly the teacher may use a single unit for a single lesson. Secondly, each unit has the potential to be developed in greater depth to form the basis of a series of lessons. Finally, the book can provide a number of starting points which teachers may take forward in their own ways.

Each theme contains 5 units and each unit has a structure consisting of:
- Exploring the ideas.
- Making the dance.
- Sharing the work.
- Possible developments.

We have begun the book with a theme which introduces basic concepts, such as actions, space and dynamics, taught through the use of the senses. Other themes are designed to link with popular topics and can add another dimension to classroom-based learning.

The drawings are taken from work done by the authors with young people on the particular Unit to which they refer. They are included to illustrate for teachers some of the many ways in which the tasks can be interpreted. A glossary has been included to clarify some of the terms in the book.

We hope the book will offer some different approaches for teachers and generate some new ideas for the future.

Anne Allen and Janis Coley
Surrey
June 1996

DANCE for ALL 1

Anne Allen and Janis Coley

David Fulton Publishers
London

Published in association with the Roehampton Institute London

David Fulton Publishers Ltd
2 Barbon Close, London WC1N 3JX

First published in Great Britain by
David Fulton Publishers 1996

British Library Cataloguing in Publication Data

A catalogue record for this book is available from the British Library

ISBN 1-85346-437-6

Typeset by The Harrington Consultancy Ltd London N1
Printed in Great Britain by Bell & Bain Ltd, Glasgow

The Value of Dance in Education

Dance has a great deal to offer in the all-round development of young children, who essentially learn by doing. Through dance, they explore the world with their bodies, minds, senses and imaginations in an integrated and enjoyable way. Dance is a natural and spontaneous activity and dance teaching allows children to gain physical control and co-ordination as well as understanding, sensitivity and the ability to create their own dances. They learn to master an art form which threads its way through everyday life and also marks the special occasions in many cultures.

We believe:

● Dance contributes to the child's personal growth, developing the mind, body and senses in a unique way.
● All pupils have a right to be educated in dance through methods and content which are most appropriate for their needs.
● Children should feel that the work is their own, and have the freedom to experiment within the safe environment of the dance lesson.
● Learning about dance consists of learning to make dances, perform, watch and understand them.

Young children communicate through movement naturally and spontaneously. From the first movements of a new-born child to the deliberate responses of children as they interact with others, movement is a part of all of us. Hence its importance in cultural life.

Motor skills, both fine and gross, control, co-ordination and flexibility are integral to dance. Young children are in touch with their bodies intuitively and that sense needs to be developed and not lost. All learning initially takes place through the senses: the baby explores its world through, for example, touch, taste and hearing. Through sensory perceptions, the body is the point of reference for our interaction with the environment. Children make sense of what is happening as they dance by tuning into the messages from their bodies, their senses and the surroundings.

As feelings are registered through the senses, so education of the senses will result in a greater awareness of the ways in which movement can be expressive. The development of this ability is crucial to children's artistic and aesthetic education, whether they are making, performing or watching dance.

Cognitive skills develop simultaneously. For example, the understanding of concepts and the ability to recall are central to learning and also allow children, when they are dancing, to visualise, reflect, interpret, imagine and create. The expressive use of language can be developed through dance by the teachers' choice of vocabulary and the way in which children are encouraged to discuss and describe the work.

In addition to what children learn individually, they also learn to work with others. Again movement is the medium through which they explore relationships with other children and the teacher.

Beyond the school environment, dance is a powerful element in most cultures, it provides opportunities to come to understand other people and their customs. Appreciating each other's dance, from an informal sharing at the end of the lesson to giving and watching performances, helps in the development of children's social skills.

The importance of dance in education is multi-faceted. Its richness lies in the way it builds on children's natural love of movement and contributes to their all-round development as well as to their social and cultural education.

Learning in Dance

For young children, the dance lesson is primarily experiential. Physical activity is central to the learning. Children should have opportunities to create their own dances and to observe and reflect on their own work as well as that of others. The three-stranded approach of making, performing and appreciating is an established model for teaching dance and is a requirement of the National Curriculum for physical education which includes dance.

Each strand makes certain demands on children and develops important skills which are transferable. The dancer uses the three strands simultaneously, planning and reflecting are ongoing parts of performing and making dances. Therefore it is important that teaching is shaped to develop all the strands from the outset in an integrated way.

Dance making is the process of putting together movements with the ultimate aim of composing whole dances, however short. On a basic level it involves making choices about movements. From the simplest decisions children make about their own actions, for example, what part of the body to turn on, to making dances with others, the choices remain essentially the same. Children will need to decide how and where to move, and perhaps more complexly, how to combine more than one idea in their partner or group dance. They are learning to create a unified whole appropriate to the stimulus they have been given.

The role of the teacher is to help pupils to develop a number of skills such as experimenting with ideas, considering them and selecting the most suitable. It is important to allow time for children to work through these stages and for them to use their imaginations in seeking innovative interpretations of the task.

Social skills are equally important. In lessons, children will be working alongside others, sharing the space, exchanging their ideas and dancing together. This will require children to show an awareness and acceptance of others. These are fundamental interpersonal skills.

Performance skills include the basic actions of travelling, jumping, turning, gesture and stillness, and movement qualities, that is, changes of flow, energy and speed. The teacher needs to provide challenges for children to improve the control, co-ordination and quality of the movements, and to gain awareness of how to use the space. Performing or doing may consist of dancing for others to watch during lessons or a more formal performance when the work is presented to a wider audience. Mastering these skills can support a positive self-image and increase confidence as the pupils become more competent, through encouragement and frequent opportunities to show their work.

Learning to refine the processes of making and performing dance depends on the third strand of appreciation. Children will need to reflect on their work as they perform and remember what they have done in order to improve. Above all, this strand aims to foster an appreciation of quality by the pupil.

The first skill is learning to observe certain elements to which the teacher draws attention; for example, children may be asked to look for the different ways of jumping. This stage is reinforced by questions from the teacher, such as asking children how the jumps varied, and followed by opportunities to implement in practice. Further phases of the observation would be to describe what has been seen and then to make comparisons. Through observing, pupils will gain a sense of what contributes to quality in dance, which should enhance their own dance making and performing.

It is important that pupils feel free to make their own decisions and are not hampered by anticipating what the teacher expects them to say. If the climate of the lesson is supportive, that is, if pupils feel free to speak, knowing their views have been heard and respected, they will gain confidence in their own judgements, and this in turn will encourage their creative responses. Evaluating dance is not a simple or passive process of observation and in the last resort, children will place an interpretation on the dance as a result of their own experience and perceptions.

Such full and active involvement in the lesson is an important factor in developing pupils' capacity to evaluate in dance.

The integrated approach, with all three strands contributing to the learning process, will help the children to develop a valuable range of skills both within the dance lesson and beyond.

Glossary

The glossary offers an explanation of some of the terms used in the book as we explain **WHAT** dance actions are, **HOW** the body moves, **WHERE** the dancers move to, the **RELATIONSHIPS** which have to be considered and **WHY** this particular dance is being made.

WHAT

● *PARTS OF THE BODY* – The body can be moved as a whole or certain parts can be emphasised.
Example: clapping with the knees.

● *BODY DESIGN* – The way the dancer chooses to shape the body in movement or stillness.
Examples: curled, thin, tall, twisted.

● *TRAVEL* – Moving into another part of the space on any part(s) of the body.
Examples: creep, jog, slither, dash.

● *GESTURE* – Actions where part or all of the body bends, stretches or twists, without travelling.
Examples: fold, pat, jerk, push, pull.

● *STILLNESS* – The body is actively held still.
Examples: freeze, hover, pause.

● *JUMP* – The whole body takes off from and returns to the floor.
Examples: bounce, hop, fly.

● *TURN* – Actions which cause the whole body to face a different direction.
Examples: spin, rotate, spiral.

Combinations of these actions – for example, stretching while turning and any variations – form the fabric of the dance.

HOW

How the body moves will begin to give the movement particular qualities, sometimes referred to as dynamics. The quality is what makes the movement expressive.

- *TIME* – Pace, changes of speed, rhythm and phrasing.
Examples: racing, hurrying, slowing, dawdling.

- *ENERGY* – Different degrees of body tension or power.
Examples: stiff, floppy, heavy, floating.

- *FLOW* – Whether the action is performed freely and continuously or in a more contained way.

WHERE

All the ways in which the dancer uses the space.

- *LEVELS*
Examples: high, low, in the middle space.

- *DIRECTIONS*
Examples: forwards, backwards, sideways.

- *PATHWAYS* – These can be on the floor or the pathway which the movement traces in the air.
Examples: jumping along a zig-zag pathway, drawing a circle in the air.

RELATIONSHIP

The relationship may be between parts of the body, the dancer and an object or one or more of the dancers.
Examples: near to/far from, above/below, at the same time/one after the other, matching/contrasting.

WHY

The dance will be shaped by the dancer's intentions. How (s)he moves will be influenced by the attitude and what the dance is about, which may be to communicate an idea, or purely for the sensation of enjoying moving in space.

Theme 1 Making Sense

1.1 Squeeze, Wobble, Melt

The qualities of **how** actions are performed transform movement into dance. The opening unit explores two dimensions, the range of body tension and changes of speed, which can contribute towards the expressiveness of the movement.

Resources

1. A list of action words which suggest degrees of tension or speed.
2. Music: 'Sheep Lie'. *Wonderful World of Percussion.* Emil Richards CD 914.

Exploring the ideas

Squeeze

1 Sit down and slowly squeeze your fingers together to make your hand into a fist. Look at how your hand is moving as you do it. Make your hand so strong that no one could open it.

Teaching point
Because we have greater control of using the hands, focusing on them first will give children the physical experience of squeezing, as well as reinforcing the effects visually.

2 Imagine your arms are giant fingers and squeeze these into your chest.

3 Repeat the action but this time squeezing your whole body together. Curl your back and head in at the same time making your body really strong as you do it.

4 Now stand up and use your arms, legs and head as your five fingers and try to squeeze them all together. Use your tummy and back muscles to help you.

Teaching points
(a) Still doing the action slowly will emphasise how the action is performed rather than the shape made.

(b) Concentrating on using the muscles in the torso is essential to a good performance.

5 Can you travel around your own space squeezing into the floor as you move?

Teaching points
(a) Here the gesture is developed into travelling, the quality still being more important than the action.
(b) Remind children to release the tension between each action in order to regain the feeling of strength.

6 Lie down and let your whole body go floppy, as though all the energy has gone from your muscles.

Teaching points
(a) This is an opportunity to explain to pupils that their muscles have been using energy as they pulled up tight and now need to release the tension.
(b) It is important to gauge when the children need moments of relaxation during the lesson. This encourages children also to become attuned to the messages their bodies are giving them.

Squeezing the body

Wobble

1 Stand up and, keeping your body loose, can you make your back, bottom and tummy move quickly? Let your arms hang by your sides and move freely.

Teaching point
Encourage children to concentrate on the loose quality rather than making the action fast. This should provide a clear contrast between the strong use of tension in the squeezing action.

2 Move around in the same way but sometimes travelling, sometimes turning. Can you also wobble as you jump? Imagine you are a flying jelly.

Teaching points
(a) Certain movement qualities are more easily experienced in particular actions. It is by asking children to develop these qualities through a range of actions which will extend their movement vocabulary and give them increasing control of their bodies.
(b) Applying the qualities to more demanding actions allows the teacher to differentiate by task.

Melt

1 Kneel on the floor and slowly let your body relax until you slide down to a lying position. Try different ways of doing this remembering always to keep the movements slow and relaxed.
2 Now start a little higher from the ground. Let your knees melt first, followed by hips, backs then shoulders.

Teaching point
The process of giving in to gravity should be relaxed but still controlled and therefore slow.

Making the dance

Choose one movement each for squeezing, wobbling and melting. Join them together to make your dance sentence. Remember you must always start and end your dance with stillness.

Teaching point
The children may choose whether to gesture, jump, travel or turn but the emphasis should be on how the movements are performed.

The teacher's own notes

Sharing the work

The whole class performs to the teacher who then selects the best examples for each quality for the class to watch.

Possible developments

Other words which suggest use of tension and speed can be used.

1.2 Making Shapes

Stillness and clear body design are integral parts of dance. Learning to copy shapes, taken from drawn figures, in different ways is explored in this unit.

Resources

1. Enough paper plates with a variety of pin men figures drawn on them for each child to have one.
2. Music: 'Air a Danser'. Penguin Café. Orchestra. Virgin EEGCD 11.

Exploring the ideas

1 Look at the shape of the pin man on your plate. Find a space and see if you can make your body into that shape and hold very still.

Teaching point

Help the children to look at detail, that is, which way the head is turned, and to realise that the shape is essentially two dimensional although some licence may be necessary, depending on the experience of the children.

2 Now turn the plate round and see if you can make the shape with your body in any other way, sideways on or maybe even upside down. Remember your best ideas.

Teaching point

Rotate the plate vertically at first, the idea of turning it as if it were a clock face may help the children to remember this.

3 Now put the plate down flat and try out the shape lying on the floor.

Teaching point

This introduces the concept or working in different planes which is important in dance but difficult for young children to grasp. Using the plate offers a concrete way of demonstrating this.

4 Starting in the shape find a way of moving to a different level, so if you are starting on the floor you will finish with your shape high up and vice versa. Now start in the same way, but this time travel away from your place and back again.

Teaching points

(a) Moments of stillness act as punctuation in movement sentences, giving phrasing and clarity. It may be necessary to work on moving into and out of the shapes fluently; using expressions such as melting, freezing or crystallising may help.

(b) Linking actions may be jumps, turns or ways of travelling.

(c) Travelling away from the spot and back may be in forwards/backwards directions, from one side to the other or combinations of these. These may be best established by reminding children which part of the body is leading the action, e.g. the chest/back and then sides of the body.

Trying to copy

Making the dance

Choose at least two ways of showing the shape ideas you have and decide how you are going to link them. Remember to move in different levels and directions as you make your dance.

Teaching points

(a) Although the main focus of learning is to create the still shapes from a visual stimulus, the links are important to the finished dance phrase.

(b) Repeating the phrase will give a pattern which could be further developed by enlarging the linking movements each time.

Sharing the work

Show your dance to a partner, making sure that you make the shapes clearly and hold them absolutely still. Ask him or her to check whether the shapes match the plate design. Change over.

Teaching points

(a) The clarity of shape will be checked by partners who should then be encouraged to give constructive help.

(b) Select some children who have achieved clear shapes and fluent, logical links to demonstrate again. Ask observers to notice how they move between the shapes.

Possible developments

◇1◇ Working in twos, pupils can find ways of linking the shapes together, as in a piece of sculpture, linking the shapes by moving away from and towards each other.

◇2◇ Develop the dance phrases by working in twos or threes and learning each other's patterns.

The teacher's own notes

1.3 Percussion

Percussion instruments are a rich source of dance ideas. Here percussion sounds provide both the stimulus and accompaniment for the dance.

Resources

An assortment of percussion instruments, e.g. chime bars, Chinese bells, cymbals, maracas, tambours, tambourines, triangles, beaters, wood blocks, enough for at least one between two pupils.

Exploring the ideas

⒈ Sit in a circle and see what sounds you can make with the instrument you have been given. If you do not have an instrument at the moment you can suggest different ways of making a sound to the person sitting next to you.

Teaching points

(a) Instruments should be distributed evenly among the circle.

(b) At this stage let the children 'play' at making sounds.

(c) A signal or instruction to STOP is advisable, one which all class members can see or hear easily.

(d) Sitting in the circle yourself and joining in at this stage will help establish a sharing activity.

⒉ Now pass your instrument to the person next to you and let him or her experiment with different sounds. If you have been given another instrument, you can continue to find different sounds with this.

Teaching points

(a) Suggestions as to how to make a variety of sounds may be given but avoid directing children to respond in a prescribed way.

(b) Repeat the process of practising with them passing on the instruments until all children have had several turns.

⒊ Find a space in the room and listen to the sound being made. Can you find a movement that matches the sound. Is it a sharp or smooth sound? Is it strong or soft?

Teaching point

Select one instrument to play at a time.

⒋ Now make your movements last as long as the sound.

Teaching point

Choose ways of playing the instruments that resound or ones where the sound is short and sharp.

⒌ Join with a partner and decide who is going to play the instrument first and who is going to move first. Players, you must choose two sounds then play them several times over while your partner practises his or her movements to dance the sounds. Dancers, are you making sure your movements are like the sounds being played, and that you make them last a long time or do them very quickly?

Teaching points

(a) Allocate instruments randomly or give less versatile instruments to creative pupils.

(b) Ensure both partners take a fair turn at both player and dancer.

(c) Partners need to work near each other.

Exploring sounds

Making the dance

Play your chosen sounds three times while your partner performs his or her dance sentence. Dancers, find a still shape to begin which shows the type of movement you are going to start with. Is the beginning of your dance sharp or smooth? Strong or soft? Does it begin slowly or do you move suddenly? Find a still position at the end of the sounds. Change over.

Sharing the work

One pair watches another and decides whether the movement matches the accompaniment. The teacher then selects one or two pairs to perform to the class.

Possible developments

〈1〉 In fours, one percussionist using two instruments while the other three dancers perform.

〈2〉 Translate a story into dance. (See Unit 4.1, Chinese New Year, page 32).

The teacher's own notes

1.4 Spin, Stick, Slide

Body awareness is developed through contact with the floor using these actions.

Resources

Music: 'Underdog Rag'. *Wonderful World of Percussion.*
Emil Richards Interworld CD 914.

Exploring the ideas

1 Find which parts of the body you can spin on.

Teaching points

(a) Children may need help in realising it is only possible to spin on clothing, not skin.

(b) SAFETY: Remind children to reverse the spin to avoid becoming dizzy.

See how many turns you can make with one pushing action only.

Teaching points

(a) Children may need to be told to prepare by twisting the body away from the direction of spin first.

(b) Rotation will be helped by holding the body tense in a particular body shape.

2 Now experiment with sliding, again on different parts of the body.

Teaching points

(a) Originality of response will depend on which part of the body is in contact with the floor and whether the arms, legs or trunk are used to drive the action.

(b) Transfer of information learnt in spinning, e.g. clothing in contact with the floor, preparation for the action and how far one push can take them, will help.

3 Now try gripping the floor with different parts of your body touching it as if you are stuck like glue. Hold yourself stiffly and strongly so that no one could move you. Find some unusual positions to get stuck in.

Teaching point

Encourage children to use surfaces of the body other than hands, feet and knees.

Making the dance

Choose a spinning action followed by one of your ways of sticking. From this you are going to perform one of the slides you have practised and finish with another way of sticking.

Teaching point

Emphasise the need for children to plan how they will be able to get from one action to another fluently. This may determine their choice of actions and shapes.

Sharing the work

Whole class performs for the teacher who then selects a few to show good examples of work to the class. The remaining pupils then have the chance to repeat their dance and improve on it.

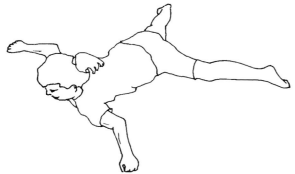
Gripping the floor

Possible developments

A dance using the tactile responses of pushing and pulling against the floor or possibly a partner.

1.5 Copy Me

Young children identify first with the teacher who can introduce them to simple rhythms, actions and ways of using different parts of the body through this unit. In time, working with others will grow from this. Additionally, learning to watch and to copy are fundamental to dancing with others. Watching, processing the information, remembering and repeating skills can be developed by practising copying the teacher. A lesson can be framed from the range of alternatives offered here depending on the needs of the class.

Resources

Music: 'Kube' and 'Hakuna Matata'.
Rhythm of the Pridelands.
Walt Disney 60871–7.

Exploring the ideas

1 Bending and straightening knees.

2 Stepping on the spot with high knees (variations – low, turned out to side).

3 Running on the spot (variations – jumping, combinations of these, e.g. eight of each, four, two, one, with turns, e.g. quarter, half, full).

4 Clapping (variations – high, low, to sides, in front, behind, near and far from body, clap with knees, elbows, feet).

5 Patting hands (variations – on floor, knees, bottoms, chests, faces, both hands together, alternately).

6 Reaching with arms leading (variations – legs or head leading, high, low, to sides, in front, behind, both arms together, alternately, taking one/two/four/eight beats each time).

Teaching points

(a) Position yourself so that every child can see and hear you.

(b) Move to different sides of the room during the lesson to ensure different children have a chance to be in the front.

(c) Remind children to keep spaced out so that everyone can see.

(d) Allow enough repetitions of each action for the children to be able to copy confidently.

Copying the teacher

Possible developments

◇1◇ Children can choose a selection of ideas and put them together as a pattern, either individually or in pairs.

◇2◇ Invite individuals to suggest movements to copy.

The teacher's own notes

Theme 2 Animals

2.1 Minibeasts

Children imagine the way in which insects might move and respond to their environment.

Resources

1. Pictures of a variety of insects.

2. Video showing minibeasts moving, e.g. David Bellamy programmes.

3. Video: *Honey! I shrunk the kids.*

4. *Minibeasts: A book of Poems* (ed. Fisher, R.). Faber and Faber.

5. Music: 'Ugly Bug Ball'. *Cartoon Time Favourites* – Rolf Harris. BBCZCR 642.

Exploring the ideas

1 Move around the room trying to keep your knees as wide apart as possible.

Teaching points
(a) Encourage children to move on different parts of their bodies, e.g. hands and feet, fronts and backs.
(b) Tummies or backs may be facing the ceiling.

2 This time, try to keep your knees together, let them touch each other as you move.

3 Can you make your elbows move together and apart as you dance?

Teaching point
Encourage the class to use all the space in the room, by moving around yourself to provide a changing focus.

4 Now try to dance using your knees and elbows moving towads each other and away again.

Teaching point
Using high and low levels with both knees and elbows will give variety.

5 Find a shape and hold it still where your knees and elbows are very important.

Teaching point
This can be likened to the way that insects will freeze sometimes as you get very near to them.

6 Jump and see if you can make the same shape in the air.

Teaching point
The priority in jumping actions is that the landings are safe and controlled, encourage resilience through the bending of ankles, knees and hips.

Making the dance

① Move about the room, using all your ideas and remembering to make knees and elbows dance together and apart. When you meet another person, freeze for a moment and then jump past him/her.

Teaching point
Children may need to be reminded of the still positions that they explored and to focus on knees and elbows.

Making elbows important

② An improvised ending for the dance.
Now imagine that a giant foot as big as the ceiling appears above you in the garden. Slowly shrink into the ground and then quickly scurry away to a safe place in the room, finishing with your favourite still shape.

Teaching points
(a) SAFETY. Children will often move towards the edges of the room when asked to find a safe place. Check that there are no

hazards and that they avoid crowding.
(b) Children may have seen the film 'Honey! I shrunk the kids!' and recall the section where the tiny children move amongst a forest of grass, threatened by every footfall.

Sharing the work

Whole class demonstrates their dance for the teacher to observe.

Teaching point
Comment on particularly lively use of the knees and elbows and on those who are imaginatively involved in the dance.

Possible developments

Using the music 'Ugly Bug Ball' take the idea of the minibeasts meeting at a party and dancing in pairs.

The teacher's own notes

2.2 Cats

The unit offers a contrast as children explore movements which are more fluid, and the characteristic stillness, pouncing and playful actions of cats.

Resources

1. Children's descriptions of their family cats.

2. Music: 'Overture'. *CATS*. Andrew Lloyd Webber. Polydor CATXC001. 'Pink Panther'. *Greatest Hits*. James Galway. RCA RK87778.

Exploring the ideas

1 Practise stretching and curling up on the spot. Can you arch and round your back like a cat?

Teaching points

(a) Beginning on hands and knees helps children to focus on how the spine is used.

(b) Remind children to use their necks too so that their heads move in line with their spines.

2 Curl up like a cat, making your whole body rounded and then stretch out as if you are ready for action!

Teaching point

Encourage a variety of starting positions by reminding children to try different parts of the body in contact with the floor and to use different levels.

3 Move around the room, softly and smoothly like a cat on the prowl, pausing now and then to look around.

Teaching points

(a) Remind children that cats move silently because they place their feet carefully and keep their whole bodies flexible.

(b) Encourage travelling on the feet as well as hands, feet and knees, whilst keeping the quality of the action.

4 Stop and stay still in your cat shape. Turn to a partner and stare at him or her without moving a whisker!

Teaching point

This could be linked with the travelling so that children stop and stare at anyone else that they meet.

5 Can you spring lightly and as fast as lightning, like a cat pouncing?

Teaching points

(a) SAFETY: Children may attempt to spring and land on their hands. If so, begin with small springs and emphasise correct placing of the hands, i.e. fingers outspread and pointing forwards.

(b) Tensing the muscles in preparation will help in achieving a sudden spring.

Making the dance

Your dance begins and ends with your

rounded cat shape. From there, stretch, prowl around the room, staring at the others as you meet them. When you are ready, make three pouncing jumps and then finish in your chosen still position.

Teaching points

(a) Recall for the class that the use of the spine is the single most important part of the dance. Commenting to pupils who are doing that effectively as they work, or stopping to allow them to demonstrate will help.

(b) The sudden pounces should contrast sharply with the slow prowling and staring phase.

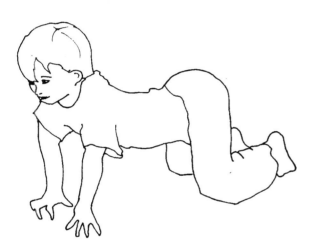

Waiting to pounce

Sharing the work

Half class demonstrations. Observers look for pupils who are really remembering to arch and round their backs throughout the dance. Select a few to demonstrate and then allow all the children one more attempt at their own dance, endeavouring to improve the way they use their spines.

Teaching point

Good use of the spine is fundamental to the

quality of children's work in dance and should be encouraged at every stage, even reminding them to sit well whilst listening or watching will help.

Possible developments

⟨1⟩ Children may suggest ideas from their own observation of cats which could develop into another section to the dance, e.g. playing with a string or a ball, rolling or stalking actions.

⟨2⟩ There are several characters from *The Old Possum Book of Practical Cats* by T.S. Eliot, which could become the basis for dances.

The teacher's own notes

15

2.3 I'm Growing Into a Frog

The study of this popular topic can be enhanced by exploring the work through dance using a video of a professional company performing *Tales of Beatrix Potter.*

Resources

1. Warner home video. *Tales of Beatrix Potter*, with dancers of the Royal Ballet. PES 3826.

2. Natural history videos of tadpoles and frogs.

3. Pictures of charts showing the development of frogspawn into tadpoles and then frogs.

4. Music: 'Pythagoras's Trousers'. Penguin Café Orchestra. Virgin EEGCD11.

Exploring the ideas

1 Frogspawn – Make yourself into a soft round shape like a blob of frogspawn. In your own space make small bouncing movements, slowly and carefully keeping your body as rounded as possible.

Teaching point

If the class is capable, this could be performed with all the children close together forming one mass.

2 Tadpoles – Try to move by wriggling your body, keeping your legs close together. Remember that small tadpoles do not have arms and legs!

Teaching point

Encouraage children to try this both on the floor and on their feet taking tiny unobtrusive steps.

3 Legs appear! Make a movement with each arm and leg in turn to show how the tadpole grows into a frog.

Teaching point

The actions could be done slowly or more humorously, sharply, accompanied by a popping sound (limited to 4) which the children make.

4 The frog – Crouch down like a frog, turning out your knees and elbows. Keep as still as you can but shoot one arm out as if to catch a passing insect.

Teaching point

Ask the children to make this gesture as sharp and sudden as possible, to contrast with the stillness of the held position. Try with one arm then the other.

5 Jumping. Look at the video and notice the different ways that Jeremy Fisher jumps.

Teaching points

(a) Use only the brief sequence of jumps in the episode before Jeremy Fisher goes fishing. The children will need to see it more than once.

(b) This preparation could be done in the classroom immediately prior to the lesson.

(c) Depending on the ability of the children, you may need to direct their observations to one or more of the following details, in order of performance difficulty:

● *One or two feet used for taking off and landing?*
● *Shape of the body in flight?*
● *Directions in which the jumps travel?*
● *How are the jumps linked into sequences?*
● *How does the dancer vary the jumps?*

Now try out some of the jumps you have been watching.

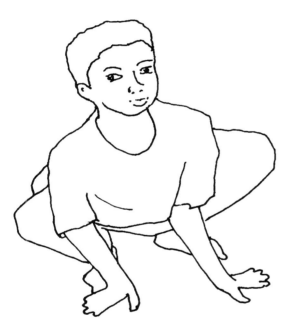

Frog shape

Making the dance

Begin close to the others in your rounded frogspawn shape, bouncing slowly and gently. Stretch out your legs gradually, keeping them together and travel, wriggling like a tadpole to a space of your own. Let your arms and legs appear, one by one. Crouch down in your frog shape and make darting

movements with first one arm and then the other. Finally, leap up and show some of the jumps you have learned from the video.

Sharing the work

Half class demonstrations.

Teaching point
Pupils should be guided to look for jumps they recognise from the video extract.

Possible developments

Other extracts from the Jeremy Fisher episode could be used to explore different movements such as fishing, falling into the water, swimming, climbing out and drying off.

The teacher's own notes

2.4 Things That Go Bump in the Night

The children's imagination is stirred to invent, through movement, creatures which may be out there in the darkness.

Resources

Music: Extracts from the *Turangalila Symphony*. Olivier Messaian RCA 09026. 'Ethnicolor'. *Images: The Best of Jean Michel Jarre*. Polydor 511306-4. Sound effects tapes, e.g. wind whistling, everyday objects which can be used for making sounds.

Exploring the ideas

Class discussion arising from the stimulus of sounds made or provided by the teacher.

1 Close your eyes and listen. Imagine you are in the dark, what sort of creature might be making these sounds? Is it friendly? What shape might it be? How big is it? How and when does it move? Choose three or four words to describe the picture in your mind.

Teaching point
Encourage the imaginative and highly descriptive use of words in the feedback.

2 Try out several still positions to show what the creature looks like. Choose the one that you think is the most unusual.

Teaching point
Comments such as 'Where are its eyes?' 'Does it have wings?' 'Legs?' 'Spikes?' will help the children to invent original shapes which involve the whole body.

3 Make one movement which shows what sort of creature you are.

Teaching points
(a) Ask the pupils to choose carefully the part of the body that they will use.
(b) The expressiveness of the movement will depend on how the movement is performed, e.g. slowly, powerfully, nervously, jerkily.

4 Now travel round the room as if you were the creature exploring this new place it finds itself in.

Teaching point
There should be a wide variety of responses. Choosing some pupils to demonstrate a range of ideas may help others to interpret the task.

Making the dance

Use your still position, movements on the spot and ways of travelling to make a short dance.

Finish the dance by making the creature get smaller and smaller as the night darkness disappears.

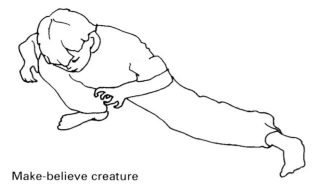

Make-believe creature

Sharing the work

Half class demonstrations.

Teaching point
Ask observers to choose the most unusual dances and if possible explain why they chose them.

Possible developments

⟨1⟩ Look at creatures which are nocturnal and the special ways they move, e.g. owls (swivelling head, swooping) and bats (opening and closing, hanging).

⟨2⟩ Make masks to represent the imaginary creatures. This could be worn for the dance, but allow sufficient range of vision for safety.

⟨3⟩ Make a sound recording to accompany the dance using percussion, voice, 'body orchestra' or 'found sounds', e.g. scratching, squeaking, squelching.

2.5 Underwater Animals

Here the dance aims to recapture the movements of a variety of creatures that live in rivers, lakes or seas.

Resources

1. Videos: *The Little Mermaid, Bedknobs and Broomsticks, Ocean World.*
2. Music: 'Oxygene'. *Images: The Best of Jean Michel Jarre.* Polydor 511 306-4. 'Under the Sea'. *The Little Mermaid* soundtrack. Pickwick DSTMC 451. Various tracks from *Ocean World.* World Wildlife Fund for Nature STA 10.
3. Pictures of fish, reefs.

Exploring the ideas

1 Show me with one hand how a fish moves through the water. Now can you use both hands? Are they making two fish or are they working together?

Teaching points

(a) Encourage the smooth, flowing qualities and the use of curving pathways.

(b) Two hands can dance together or far apart, doing the same movements or contrasting ones.

2 Can you make your arms join in the dance with the same sort of movements? Come up to standing and move your whole body in the same way. Now move round the room, slowly weaving in and out making curly pathways in the air and on the floor as though you are exploring underwater.

Teaching points

(a) Although the hands and arms are leading the movement ask pupils to use their whole bodies and to use the same curving, flowing qualities throughout.

(b) Ask the children to think about what sort of plants and objects they might find on the seabed.

3 Find your own space in the room and make yourself into a solid shape, like a rock or reef.

Teaching point

Ask the pupils to tense their muscles and feel the strength of the still shape they have chosen. Ability to use appropriate body tension is a fundamental skill in dance.

4 Keeping your body strong can you make a shape like a cave?

Teaching point

Encourage pupils to find shapes with a variety of spaces and holes. This can be achieved by using different body parts to take the weight.

5 In twos, one of you make a rock shape whilst your partner moves around you like a fish exploring. Change over. Now try with one of you making your body into a cave. Can you make spaces big enough for your partner to swim through?

Teaching points

(a) SAFETY. Emphasise strong stable cave positions. If pupils work without touching,

this avoids one causing the other to lose balance.

(b) Partners may go through with one hand or arm only depending on the size of the space.

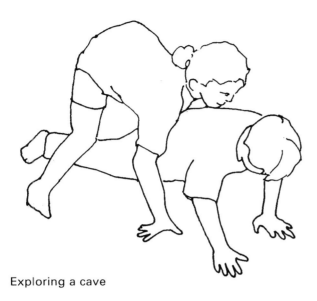

Exploring a cave

Making the dance

Decide between you who will make the rock or cave shape first and who will move like a fish. Start close together and begin with the fish exploring the rock or cave. Now you may be more adventurous and travel round the room.

Teaching points

(a) Allow only one person to dance near each rock or cave at a time

(b) Remind pupils of the flowing curving movements for the fish and the strong stillness of their partners.

Change over.

Sharing the work

Half the pairs sit out and watch the others. Ask the children to look out for dancers whose movements make them look as though they are moving through the water. Change over.

Possible developments

⟨1⟩ Discuss with children plants such as sea-anemones which have interesting movements, e.g. opening and closing. These could then be introduced as alternatives.

⟨2⟩ Use different types of underwater animals which have a range of movements, e.g. crabs scuttling sideways, eels slithering and an octopus.

The teacher's own notes

Theme 3 Autumn and Winter

3.1 Falling Leaves

The dance explores the movement of leaves as the weather changes.

Resources

1. Examples of various types of leaves in different states.
2. Pictures of trees in Summer, Autumn and Winter.
3. Music: 'Entropy' *Drummin' an' Dancin'*. Primrose Educational Resources

Exploring the ideas

1 Look at these leaves and notice how the colours have changed and how they feel different. Notice how some of them have crinkly edges and crumpled shapes.

Teaching point

Explain to your class that in Autumn, leaves dry out and this makes it possible for the wind to blow them off the trees.

2 Show me with your body how the leaves hang on the tree, and how they are made to move by the wind.

Teaching points

(a) Children should try to reflect the
crumpled, pointed or rounded shapes with their bodies.

(b) Encourage pupils to show which part of their body still suspends them.

(c) Variety can be developed through large and small swaying and swinging movements and by using the whole body, especially the spine.

3 What happens when the leaf falls? How could you describe the movement.

Teaching points

(a) Choose a leaf with a large surface to drop to the floor (it should show a drifting action).

*(b) Emphasise words which describe the **quality** of the movement, e.g. drifting, swooping, gently, silently, and the pathways, e.g. curvy, spiralling.*

4 Now see if you can continue the swaying and swinging actions but gradually move downwards to settle on the floor, shaping your body like one of the leaves.

Teaching points

(a) The dancers can begin to travel so that they finish in a different part of the room.

(b) Pupils should aim to recapture, in the

way that they move, the qualities and pathways that were described.

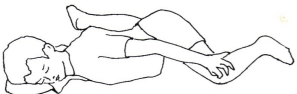

Making a leaf shape

Making the dance

Start your dance with one of your ideas for hanging on the tree and being blown by the wind. Then imagine a strong gust of wind has blown you away and finish your dance as you gradually settle on the ground.

Teaching point
Ask pupils to start with small movements and build them up to take them into a new space before they finish their dance.

Sharing the work

Half the class demonstrates for the other, which is the audience. Choose one person that you are going to watch and see if their dance reminds you of the way the leaf floated down.

Teaching point
Invite pupils to make positive comments, if they particularly liked the dance they chose to watch.

Possible developments

<u>1</u> Sweeping actions to represent brushing up fallen leaves.

<u>2</u> Kicking piles of leaves.

Both of these make lively contrasts if used in conjunction with the main work.

The teacher's own notes

3.2 Fireworks

All the basic actions of dance, jumping, turning, travelling and gesturing, together with stillness, are developed in this unit using the stimulus of fireworks.

Resources

1. Examples of types of fireworks, such as rockets, Catherine wheels, sparklers and firecrackers.
2. Music: Sound effects of fireworks. 'Yes Pulstar'. *The Best of Vangelis*. RCA PK 7011.

SAFETY: It is important that pupils are made aware of the Firework Code.

Exploring the ideas

1 Try out some jumps which explode in the air, where your body shoots upwards, fast and high, making a straight shape.

Teaching point

Encourage safe controlled landings on the feet, pupils need to realise that the tension needed to make a particular shape in the air, must be released in order to land resiliently.

2 How many different ways of turning can you find? Can you make fast turns and also turns that start slowly, speed up and die down again?

Teaching points

(a) SAFETY. Pupils need to make turns in alternate directions to avoid losing control.

(b) Turning on different parts of the body will give variety.

(c) Making the body large slows the turn down and vice versa.

3 Think about the way that showers of sparks cascade down from a sparkler or other firework. Using hands wrists and fingers, can you make fast shimmering patterns from high to low?

Teaching points

(a) Hand gestures will be emphasised if children are asked to focus on their fingers as they move.

(b) The rest of the body can be active in helping to make the action begin as high as possible and finish close to the ground.

(c) Moving at lightning speed needs body tension, this is most easily experienced with the hands.

4 Can you dodge and dart around the room, with fast steps making sudden, zig-zag actions?

Teaching point

Sharp sudden changes of direction whilst travelling will give the zig-zag pathways greater clarity.

Making the dance

Perform all four parts of your firework dance in this order:

Explosive jumps

Rocket jumps, Catherine wheels, sparkler gestures and firecracker dash.

Teaching points

(a) Teacher chooses and indicates when a new section starts.

(b) Children should try hard to make the different movements and their qualities as clear as possible.

Sharing the work

Teacher selects some pupils who have clear actions to demonstrate. Remainder of class watches and then pupils perform their own dances.

Possible developments

$\langle 1 \rangle$ A class dance to represent a bonfire.

$\langle 2 \rangle$ The story of the Gunpowder plot as a starting point.

3.3 Festival of Light

Many cultures have festivals of light as part of their tradition, e.g. Divali. Here the theme of darkness and light is explored through movement, which helps to enrich this area of study in the rest of the curriculum.

Resources

1. Candle and match, torches.

2. Pictures of light sources, sunsets, sunrises.

3. Celebrations involving light.

4. Music: 'Into the Burning Circle'. *Dancing With the Lion.* Andreas Vollenweider. CBS 463331 2.

Exploring the ideas

Class discussion

Do you know any ways in which light is used in celebrations, e.g. candles on cakes, Divali, lights in trees, Chinese lanterns? How do you feel and move when it is dark? What are the differences in the ways you can move when it is light?

Beginning in the dark

☐1 Find different starting positions so that your eyes are covered.

Teaching point
Suggest a variety of standing, sitting, lying positions, covering eyes with hands or arms.

☐2 Explore the space around you with your hands and arms, keeping your eyes shut. Reach up to standing and take some slow, careful steps around your own space.

Teaching point
Encourage children to feel the surface of the floor with their feet as they step as well as feeling the way with arms and hands.

☐3 Remember what it felt like to move in the dark. Now try to repeat that with your eyes open and feel your way to different parts of the room.

Teaching point
Ask pupils to move close to the floor and high up.

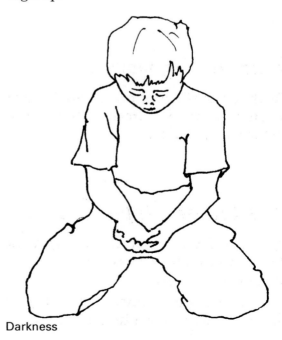

Darkness

26

Lighting the candle

1 Start with your body curled in. Slowly move upwards, curving gently from side to side, like a flame.

Teaching point
The aim is to use the whole body, making small curves which are sometimes large and sometimes small.

2 Now that it is light, move freely around the room with wide spreading movements to show how light fills the space.

Teaching point
Encourage larger, more energetic movements of turning, travelling and jumping, contrasting the wide open body shapes with the earlier sections.

3 Gradually slow down and stop, making an open curved shape to finish.

Making the dance

Join the three sections of the dance together, contrasting the closed movements with the wider freer ending.

Sharing the work

Watch a partner and notice how she or he moves in the dark. Show your partner your dance.

Possible developments

1 Extend the dance to represent the way candles are floated on water in Divali celebrations.

2 Sunrise and sunset can suggest movement ideas for a further dance.

3.4 Building a Snowman

Partner dances are choreographed from ideas of playing in the snow.

Resources

1. Pictures of snow and snowmen.
2. Music: 'Paranoinia'. *Art of Noise.* China WOMC 1010.

Exploring the ideas

[1] Can you show me a long slow stretch as though you are just waking up?

Teaching point

Encourage pupils to use their trunks and legs too, not just their arms.

[2] Imagine how excited you would be to find that it had snowed! Jump as high as you can and run quickly to another space.

Try out some ways of playing in the snow.

Teaching point

Ideas such as making patterns of footprints, snowballs, rolling in the snow.

[3] Crouch down and grow bigger, taller and fatter bit by bit as if you were a snowman which someone was building.

Teaching point

Children can make their faces grow too by puffing out their cheeks.

[4] Begin to build your snowman by rolling and carrying giant snowballs.

Teaching point

Encourage large strong actions to show the size and weight of the snowballs.

Show how you would make a snowman by scooping, pressing and patting the snow.

Teaching point

Suggest that children reach high and low, working all round their imaginary snowman.

The snowman grows

Making the dance

Begin the dance with waking, stretching and rushing out. Choose one of the snow games to play by yourself. Join a partner, one of you builds the snowman and the other starts low and gradually grows bigger as you build. Repeat the last section but change with your partner so that each of you has a turn to be the snowman.

Sharing the work

Each pair watches another. The observers will decide which version is the best and tell the dancers who should be the snowman, who should be the builder.

Possible developments

◇1◇ Snowflakes as a starting point for a dance about group shapes.

◇2◇ Melting and freezing as ideas to explore different movement qualities.

◇3◇ The snowman could come alive!

The teacher's own notes

3.5 Round Dances

The word 'carol' originally meant a round dance. The unit explores some traditional steps and circular patterns, to accompaniment of a traditional carol.

Resources

Music: 'In Dulci Jubilo'. Complete Mike Oldfield. Virgin CMOC 1. 'Deck the Halls' 'Ding Dong Merrily on High' (any version). Any folk music which has a skipping rhythm could be substituted.

Exploring the ideas

1 Can you skip anywhere in the room, keeping in time with the music?

Teaching points

(a) Encourage children to skip in straight and curving lines.

(b) Skipping sideways and backwards will add variety.

(c) SAFETY. Remind pupils to look behind them when skipping backwards.

2 This time, stand still and clap in time with the music.

3 Now, clap 8 times and skip 8 times.

Teaching point

Join in with the clapping to help pupils to establish the rhythm.

4 With a partner, take 4 skips towards each other and 4 backwards skips away.

Teaching point

Remind pupils to start at an appropriate distance from their partners.

5 Practise gallop steps to both sides. Can you change after 8 in each direction?

Teaching point

In order to change direction, pupils need to prepare to transfer the weight.

6 Find ways of skipping with your partner.

Skipping in a circle

Making the dance

① Stand in a circle next to your partner, in your group. Hold hands and do 16 gallop steps to your right. Repeat to the other side.

② Let go of hands and take 4 skips into the centre of the circle. Stand still and clap 4 times.

③ Skip backwards four times to get you back to your place and repeat the claps.
④ Join with a partner and do 16 skips round the circle to the right.

Teaching point
Choose balanced groups of eights who will work well together.

Sharing the work

Watch one circle at a time. Which group works best together?

Possible developments

There are many formations which can be taken from set dances, e.g. star, *dos-à-dos*, inner and outer circles moving in same or opposite directions.

Theme 4　Spring and Summer

4.1 Chinese New Year

This festival is widely celebrated with a variety of dances, including the famous Chinese lion dance.

Resources

1. A selection of untuned percussion, e.g. wood blocks, cymbals, Chinese bells, tambourines and beaters.
2. Videos of Chinese New Year ceremonies.
3. Literature from The Commonwealth Institute, London.

Exploring the ideas

1 Discuss the way the festival is celebrated including the belief that the lion brings good luck.

2 Lie down like a sleeping lion, wake up gradually moving your head first to look around.

Teaching point

The lion is woken by the percussion getting louder and louder.

3 Keeping the feet wide apart, take large steps and move your body from side to side, swaying like a Chinese lion. As you dance, turn your head in all directions as you look for food that is being offered. Bend and stretch your legs to step low and then high.

Teaching point

It is traditional to encourage the lion's attention by offering lettuce.

4 With your percussion instrument make quiet sounds which gradually get louder. Now join with a partner. One plays while the other dances. Can you make a simple rhythm to accompany your partner's lion dance?

Teaching point

The sound should start quietly as practised and develop into a rhythm.

Change over.

Making wide steps

Making the dance

Each dancer begins with the sleeping position, wakes gradually and performs the lion dance around the room accompanied by his or her partner's playing. The dance finishes with the lion going back to sleep.

Sharing the work

Each pair watches another and tells their classmates what they like best about their dance.

Possible developments

Other Chinese New Year traditions – e.g. dancing with ribbons and sashes, street acrobats – may provide more stimuli.

4.2 Pancake Day

Some of the actions of making pancakes are used to create a dance.

Resources

Music: 'Equinoxe'. *Images: The Best of Jean Michel Jarre.* Polydor 511 306-4.

Exploring the ideas

1 Class discussion on making pancakes to introduce the ideas of mixing, cooking and tossing.

2 Imagine you have a bowl of flour, milk and eggs. Show how you would stir it really well. Now make the actions much bigger using both arms and plenty of energy.

Teaching point
The power of the action as well as its size will help to give the impression of mixing ingredients.

3 Spin, turn and whirl about as if you were in the bowl being stirred. Show how you would rise and sink down as the ingredients were mixed.

Teaching point
Different parts of the body may be used to spin on.

4 Think about how the mixture looks as it is poured into the pan. Try to sink slowly and smoothly down to the floor in the same way.

Teaching point
The quality of the movement should provide a contrast to the previous actions.

5 As the pancake cooks, the surface bubbles. Beginning in the crouched position, with your back rounded, make little bouncing jumps.

Teaching point
Children should try to lead the jump with their backs, keeping their heads and arms low.

6 Now you are going to toss the pancake. Stand as if you are holding the frying pan with both hands and shake it side to side energetically. With one big movement, toss it as high as you can.

7 Make up your own ending. Did you catch it? Did you miss it?

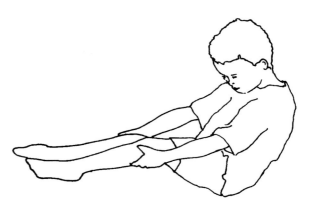

Swirling round the bowl

Making the dance

Link together your movements for stirring, pouring, bubbling, shaking and tossing into one whole dance. Don't forget to add your surprise ending.

Sharing the work

Teacher selects some children who can remember and perform the dance in the correct sequence. Observers recount the order as they watch and then perform their own.

Possible developments

Preparation of other types of food, e.g. Chinese – chop, sprinkle, stir.

The teacher's own notes

4.3 Flight

Flight is taken as the starting point for a dance about the ways in which a kite moves.

Resources

1. Balloons, pictures of birds, kites, bubbles.

2. Music: 'Oxygene 2'. Images: The Best of Jean Michel Jarre. Polydor 511 306-4

Exploring the ideas

1. Run to feel the air rush past you.

Teaching point
Organise the class into rows at one end of the room, allowing space for them to run freely and safely.

2. Run again but this time try to make your body go low and high. Change the level smoothly as you run.

Teaching point
Words like swoop, soar and dip may help.

3. This time, as well as changing the level as you run, make a curved pathway anywhere in the room, as if you are as free as the air.

Teaching point:
SAFETY: Running slowly at first will allow the children to become more aware of each other and to use the space well.

4. Now find a still position, with any part of your body touching the floor, but lift the rest of you upwards and away from the floor, hovering as though the air is supporting you.

5. Imagine you have been pulled back by the string of the kite, show this with a sudden jerk and then quickly run straight to another space in the room. Repeat the action of hovering and sudden running back to your starting position.

Teaching point
A moment of stillness in the hovering position will give a contrast with the jerk and fast running.

Up in the air

Making the dance

The whole dance consists of 4 sections – swoop, hover, jerked back and an ending of each pupil's choice.

⟨1⟩ Repeat the free, curving run, but remember where you started in the room (swoop).

⟨2⟩ Add the hover and jerking actions.

The ending can be chosen from alternatives suggested by the children, e.g. the kite escapes, gets caught or crashes.

Teaching point
Encourage contrast in the qualities of the movements, the swooping run should be light, smooth and free flowing. The jerking back is more sudden and energetic.

Sharing the work

A quarter of the class demonstrates at a time. Look for a hovering position which you really liked and copy it exactly.

Teaching point
This form of evaluation develops skills of observation and requires a simultaneous practical response from everyone rather than a verbal response from a few.

Possible developments

① Balloons as a stimulus offers the possibility of being inflated, floating, bursting or deflating.

② Bubbles will involve similar movements to those in ① but the qualities will be different, slower, lighter and more fragile.

The teacher's own notes

4.4 All the Fun of the Fair

The actions of the fairground, swinging, spinning and dipping form the basis of the unit.

Resources

1. Pictures of fairground rides.
2. Children's own experiences.
3. Music: 'Fairground'. *Seaside*. Primrose Educational Resources.

Exploring the ideas

1. On the spot, swing your arms forwards and backwards, bending your knees to make the action bigger. Now try to swing your arms around your body and then side to side.

Teaching points

(a) Encourage large movements, using the weight of the limbs to give momentum.
(b) Arms can go in the same or opposite directions.

2. Now let the swings develop into travelling, turning or jumping.

Teaching point

Allow enough time to practise this development. Increasing the size and energy of the swings should naturally lead into travelling, turning or jumping.

3. Explore ways of spinning, on different parts of the body.

Teaching points

(a) SAFETY: Remind pupils to reverse the direction of the spin each time to avoid becoming dizzy.

(b) Ask children to practise spins with their backs towards and away from the floor.

(c) The spin will be more efficient if the body is held tensely throughout. Small shapes spin faster.

4. With a partner, find ways of spinning or turning whilst holding hands.

Teaching point

Both partners may turn or one can turn the other.

5. Join with another pair and make a line, one behind the other with your hands on the shoulders of the person in front of you. Try walking first, making your group gradually rising and sinking like a group caterpillar. Now try to travel a little faster, still changing level smoothly.

Teaching points

(a) Emphasise the need to follow the actions of the person in front of you.

(b) Bending the knees to go low and rising onto the balls of the feet will help to give the sense of changing levels.

Making the dance

1. Rides that swing. Select some of your swinging actions some on the spot and some travelling. Link them together to make the first section of the dance.

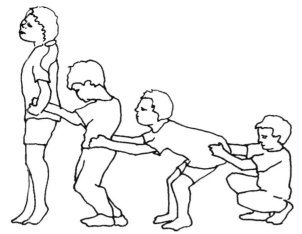

The roller-coaster

◇2◇ Rides that spin. Decide whether you want to work alone or with a partner and select your best ideas for spinning to make the middle part of the dance.

Teaching point

Children will need to plan how they make the transition between sections, including meeting up with a partner where necessary.

◇3◇ Roller coaster rides. Join with your group and move round the room in your line, changing levels like a roller coaster or big dipper. Finish by slowing down to a halt.

Teaching point

Co-operative working will be essential to the quality of this section, allow time for planning, e.g. who leads the group best? What speed should they move at? Is height order a good idea?

Sharing the work

Two groups at a time demonstrate the whole dance. Observers decide at the finish which dancers or group were the most successful at the swinging, spinning and dipping parts of the dance.

Possible developments

① The spinning pair could link with another four to spin as a group.

② Add a ghost train ending.

③ Other fairground activities – such as dodgems, hoop-la and coconut-shies – could generate different movement possibilities.

The teacher's own notes

39

4.5 May Day

A number of traditions are associated with the first of May. This unit combines two of them, the gathering of may and dancing with ribbons.

Resources

1. May day traditions.
2. Different coloured ribbons approximately 65 centimetres long for each child.
3. Music: 'The Floral Dance'. *English Heritage*. Blues and Royals Band. Pickwick DTO 10332.

Exploring the ideas

1 Sunrise. Kneel on the floor and copy your teacher by making a large circle with both arms in front of you. Make your arms stretch very high and wide.

Teaching point
The action will be larger if pupils are told to start sitting back on their heels then kneeling up as they raise their arms.

2 Gathering may blossom. Reach up as if you are picking a branch of may. Then run to a new place in the room and repeat the action. Show how big the bunch is becoming.

Teaching point
Ask pupils to make the reaching movements very clear by stretching to pick the may using different levels.

3 Making a garland. Imagine you are making a garland and arrange the blossoms carefully. Now walk around the room carrying your garland carefully and showing it to everyone you pass.

Teaching point
Explain to the class what a garland is. One example is the half-hoop shape which can be carried over the head.

4 Ribbon dance. Take your ribbon and practise making patterns in the air, high, low and all around your body. Now skip around the room filling the space with your ribbon patterns.

Teaching point
Ribbons can be placed together on the floor in one part of the room.

Making the dance

Start your dance kneeling and make your sun circles three times. On the third one stand up ready to begin the next section. Gather the may, make your garland and show it to other class mates. Then pick up your ribbon and skip lightly around the room using the air patterns you have practised. Finish the dance standing still and holding the ribbon high in the air.

Teaching point
(a) Guide the children when to start each section.

40

Dancing with a ribbon

(b) Encourage the contrast in movement between the careful stage of preparing the garland and the celebratory skipping.

Sharing the work

Half class demonstrations. Also, if possible, show the dance to another class, the rest of the school or parents.

Possible developments

① A Maypole dance.

② A partner dance based on Morris dancing.

③ Make garlands and dance with them.

④ Other traditional events such as the hobby-horse and street entertainment.

Theme 5 Myself

5.1 What Shall We Wear Today?

The lesson is based on the movements associated with getting dressed to go out on a rainy day.

Resources

Music: 'Orient Express'. Images: The Best of Jean Michel Jarre. Polydor 511306-4.

Exploring the ideas

☐ It is a rainy day and you have to decide what to wear. Copy your teacher doing the following movement pattern 'Point' (as if you are considering an item of clothing) 'Think' (a still position to show that you are making up your mind) 'Shake your head three times' (as if you have decided against that item).

Teaching points

(a) Aim to use a steady rhythm: ☐ *(point)* ☐ *(think)* ☐ *AND* ☐ *(shake head).*

(b) Encourage pupils to look as they point and to make large emphatic movements by using the whole body.

Repeat the pattern four times, pointing at a different level each time and reach forward as if you have at last decided.

☐ Imagine that you are putting on large pair of wellingtons, show how you would have to pull hard to get them on each foot in turn.

Teaching point

The starting position could be lying, sitting or standing.

Now put on your coat, does it have buttons? A zip? Run to a new space in the room, ready to jump into puddles.

Teaching points

(a) Make sure that children show the actions clearly, using both arms and enlarging the actions.

(b) Large bouncy strides would suggest running in wellingtons.

☐ Practise jumping on two feet in your own space. Can you now jump in different directions, as if you were jumping in and out of puddles? Now run to a new space and repeat your jumps in a different puddle.

☐ Imagine that the rain has made the ground very muddy. Show how you would walk if you were trying to move through deep mud.

Teaching point
Ask pupils to use strong pulling actions with arms and legs, away from the floor until each foot in turn is released.

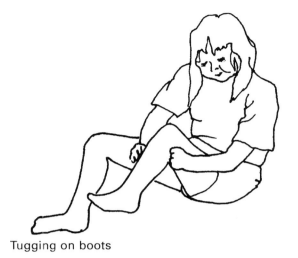
Tugging on boots

Making the dance

Begin the dance with the pointing and thinking pattern, following the teacher's timing. Then show putting on your wellingtons and coat and jumping in and out of puddles. Finish the dance with four large strides through the mud.

Teaching point
Pupils could finish the dance by falling and being 'stuck in the mud'.

Sharing the work

Whole class performs for the teacher.

Possible developments

⟨1⟩ Ring the changes by choosing different kinds of clothing and different actions to suit different types of weather.

⟨2⟩ Exploratory work based on choosing different garments from a dressing up box and finding appropriate actions.

The teacher's own notes

5.2 The Toy Cupboard

Learning how to use different degrees of body tension is an important skill in dancing expressively. This unit explores a range of ideas to encourage pupils to practise this through the stimulus of different toys.

Resources

1. Video: *The Wizard of Oz* excerpt showing the tin man.

2. Suitable toys brought in by the children or supplied by the teacher.

3. Music: 'Good Grief'. *The World of Percussion*. Emil Richards. Interworld CD914.

Exploring the ideas

☐1 Can you walk really stiffly like a robot and then turn sharply to repeat your stiff walk to somewhere else in the room?

Teaching point

Encourage sharp, angular movements by emphasising the movement of different joints.

☐2 Now you are a soft, floppy toy made of fabric which cannot stand up without flopping down. Lift one arm above your head and let it flop back into place with a relaxed, heavy movement. Now repeat this with the other arm, then the top half of your body. Finally try relaxing the knees too so that you slowly flop right down to the floor.

Teaching point

Using different directions, e.g. forwards, backwards and sideways will give variety to the responses.

How do you think floppy toys might walk?

Teaching point

Emphasising the heavy relaxed qualities of the movement will give a contrast to the robotic style.

☐3 Now you are a Jack-in-the-box. Crouch down and make yourself really small. When the teacher claps her or his hands, spring as high into the air as you can and make a wide stretched body shape.

Robot and floppy doll

Teaching point

Keeping the body tense in the crouched position will enable the children to make their springs sudden and high.

Making the dance

Choose whether you want to move like a robot or a floppy toy. Find a starting shape to show which of these you have chosen. One group will be still whilst the other shows its dances. When the teacher tells you to begin, do your chosen movements on the spot and moving around the room. Stop and hold your still position whilst the others perform.

Teaching points

(a) Keep each section short enough for the children to be able to maintain stillness in their chosen character.

(b) How the actions are performed are more important here than the movements themselves. The strong, jerky quality of the robots and the relaxed floppy style of the others should contrast.

To finish the dance, crouch down ready to do your Jack in-the-box spring when you hear the teacher clap his/her hands.

Sharing the work

One group, either the robots or the floppy dolls, watches the other and vice versa.

Teaching point

Ask each child to choose the person who uses his or her body tension best, to show the quality of the movements. Select pupils to comment.

Possible developments

⟨1⟩ The use of body tension in moving like a string puppet.

⟨2⟩ Toys which stretch and recoil or bend also offer possibilities.

⟨3⟩ Contrasting qualities can be used to make a dance with one or two other people, each person taking a different character.

The teacher's own notes

5.3 Going Out to Play

The traditional activity of hopscotch is taken to extend children's ability to jump in a variety of ways and to develop a sense of rhythm through movement.

Resources

1. Playground markings or diagram of hopscotch.
2. Music: 'Eye of a Needle'. *Art of Noise*. China – WOLMC 1010.

Exploring the ideas

1 Who could show the class how to play hopscotch? What sort of jumps are they using? Now see if you can copy them.

Teaching point

The pattern consists of jumping from two feet to one and then back to two without grounding the free foot.

2 Now try some of these jumps: hopping (one foot to the same), leaping (one foot to the other) and bouncing (two feet to two feet).

Teaching point

Introduce one jump at a time and only as many variations as the children are capable of learning.

Making the dance

Can you make a pattern by repeating some of these jumps so that you travel along a line, turn and come back again?

Teaching points

(a) Pupils may use only two types of jumps and travel simply there and back. More able pupils could be asked to extend the task by using more of the jumps, adding turns and changes of direction, whilst on their forwards and backwards pathway.

(b) Once the patterns are established, encourage children to work to a steady rhythm, either that of the music or by clapping their hands as they jump.

Hopscotch

Sharing the work

Work in twos, take it in turn to perform your dance. Your partner will try to clap the rhythm of your jump pattern. Have several turns.

Teaching point

(a) Ask pupils to tell you if their partner had a clear rhythm to their dance.

(b) Ask pairs to demonstrate where the rhythm of the dance and the accompaniment were clear.

Possible developments

⟨1⟩ Combining stepping and jumping patterns will extend the dance.

⟨2⟩ Take partner clapping games as a basis.

⟨3⟩ Other traditional activities, such as skipping games and rhymes, could be explored in a similar way.

5.4 Tidy Up Time!

Repeating actions such as lifting, carrying, pushing and polishing go to make up the patterns of this dance.

Resources

Music: 'Calypso1'. *Images: The Best of Jean Michel Jarre.* Polydor 511306-4. 'The Typewriter'. *Lusher Side of Brighouse and Rastrick Band.* Grosvenor GRS 1050.

Exploring the ideas

1 Imagine you have to tidy up the room very very quickly. Some objects are large and heavy so that you can only just carry them, moving slowly. Pile the objects up or put them in a drawer or a cupboard, before you rush to collect another one. Make your movements show what you are carrying.

Teaching points

(a) The shape of the body can indicate the size and weight of the object.

(b) Ask pupils to contrast the way they rush about to the more careful carrying movements.

1 The cupboard or drawer is bulging full! Show how you would have to push very hard to close it.

2 Now it is time to dust or polish! Make circling movements to show this.

Teaching point

The children can be encouraged to think about the surfaces they might dust, e.g. floor, mirrors, furniture and to show this by varying the levels and size of the circular actions.

Making the dance

Choose four objects, some heavy some light, some large and some small, which you are going to put away. Imagine that they are in different parts of the room as you hurry to tidy up.

Now push the drawer or the cupboard closed and begin your polishing actions. Show when you have finished with a big stretch and sigh. Stop at the end of your stretch, this is the finishing position for your dance.

Reaching a high shelf

Sharing the work

Quarter class demonstrations. Observers should look for dancers who have plenty of variety in their movements.

Possible developments

Studying the work of people who help us, e.g. window cleaners, crossing supervisors, school cleaners and cooks could offer a range of different working actions.

5.5 Up the Wooden Hill

Poems are a rich source of ideas for dance as the way language is used stimulates the imagination.

Resources

Poem: Brushing my teeth. (See below.)

Exploring the ideas

1 Listen to the poem and notice the different actions mentioned.

Teaching point

Ask the children which ones they remember.

2 Show me how you brush your teeth before you go to bed. Try making the actions go up and down, side to side, then round and round. Now do it again with the other hand.

Teaching point

Ask the class to do the movements small the first time then repeat them much larger.

3 Imagine you have hair that is very long and show how you would comb it carefully. Make long, curving movements with your hand, starting at the top of your head and pulling gently downwards.

4 You are now tired and ready for bed. Slowly climb the stairs as if every step is an effort and that you can just about put one foot in front of the other.

Teaching point

Lifting the feet slowly and heavily will give the effect of tiredness.

5 Next stretch arms and legs as wide as you can, arching your back as you do so. Repeat, stretching your whole body in another direction. Then slowly sink to the floor and find your sleeping position.

Teaching point

Encourage the children to stretch in different directions and to consider the shape of the body in their final positions.

Brushing teeth

50

Making the dance

① Taking the following phrase as a chant, make the brushing teeth actions fit the rhythm of the words: 'Up and down and side to side, round and round and round again.'

Teaching point

Saying the words slowly allows time for the children to make large actions.

② Then follow the stages of the poem, changing from one action to another when you teacher tells you.

Sharing the work

Whole class demonstrates and the teacher selects the best examples for other pupils to watch.

Possible developments

Other poems with potential for dance, including the children's own work.

Brushing my Teeth

I'm brushing my teeth,
Brush, brush.
I'm combing my hair,
Comb, comb.
I'm going to bed.
Creep, creep.
I'm in bed,
Yawn, yawn.
I'm asleep.

The teacher's own notes

Theme 6 Journeys

6.1 We're Going on a Journey

Discovering different places to play is the idea for this dance.

Resources

1. Pictures of different types of terrain.

2. The rhyme 'We're going on a journey'. (See below.)

Exploring the ideas

Climbing the hill

Walk around with giant steps. Now can you lean forward as you take your steps as if you are struggling to walk up a steep hill? Use your arms to help you.

Teaching point
Pupils may choose to swing the arms to help them or to travel on all fours.

Rolling down

[1] Lie on the floor and roll sideways, so slowly that you roll smoothly and with no sound.

Teaching point
The action is done in slow motion for safety.

[2] Now can you change the shape of the body as you roll as though you were tumbling out of control?

Through a tunnel

Try to travel with you body low down, close to the floor as if you were squeezing your way through a narrow twisting tunnel.

Teaching points
(a) Using shoulders, back and hips will help the twisting actions.
(b) Facial expressions will also help to show the effort.

Stepping stones

Stand on one leg and try to keep your balance as you make a step to the next stone. Repeat this, placing your feet carefully as if you are trying not to fall in the water.

Teaching point
Outstretched arms to the side will assist the balance.

A hiding place

Find a still body shape to show that you are hiding away. Keep very still.

Teaching point
A variety of responses will be encouraged by varying the shape of the body, the focus, the body parts in contact with the floor.

Making the dance

Perform all the actions in the order of the rhyme as your teacher reads it out finishing by doing all the movements again but in reverse order this time.

Teaching point
Read the rhyme at a pace you think is appropriate to the children's movement.

Stepping stones

Sharing the work

All demonstrate for the teacher to watch.

Possible developments

⟨1⟩ Variations on the journey rhyme that the children might suggest.
⟨2⟩ Other rhymes with actions.

We're Going on a Journey

We're going on a journey, a journey, a journey,
We're going on a journey, to see what we can find.

We're going up a big hill, a big hill, a big hill,
We're going up a big hill, I can climb.

Now we're coming down again, down again, down again,
Now we're coming down again, watch me roll.

Now it's through a tunnel, a tunnel, a tunnel,
Now it's through a tunnel, you have to be small.

Here are some stepping stones, stepping stones, stepping stones,
Here are some stepping stones, don't fall in!

We've found a secret hiding place, hiding place, hiding place,
We've found a secret hiding place, keep very still.

It's time to go home again, home again again, home again,
It's time to go home again, so...........

It's over the stepping stones, through the tunnel, up the hill and down the other side. PHEW!

The teacher's own notes

6.2 Magic Carpet Ride

Here the children's vivid imaginations are brought into play when they are asked to envisage flight by magic. Who knows where it may end?

Resources

1. The magic carpet scene from the film *Aladdin*.
2. Music: 'Jupiter'. *The Planets Suite*. Gustav Holst.

Exploring the ideas

[1] Chose your own space in the room and mark out the size of your carpet by walking around it.

Teaching point

Children need to share the space fairly.

[2] Sit or kneel on your carpet and put your hands on the floor to steady you. Look over the edge as though you are peering down from a great height. Now stretch to look over another edge. Show me by the way you do this that you are really looking down on the world.

Teaching point

This will be helped by telling the children to use their backs to stretch as they look.

[3] Now move your body from side to side as if your carpet has taken off. Sway gently to begin then still sitting or kneeling, show how your carpet rises and sinks. As you fly look all around at the wonderful sights you are passing.

Teaching points

(a)Teachers may want to ask some pupils what they might see.

(b) Asking the children to imagine how their bodies would move if the carpet tipped or swooped will help to achieve appropriate movement responses.

[4] Stand up and make the swaying, rising and sinking movements even bigger until you begin to travel like the carpet itself, spinning, whirling and jumping.

Teaching points

(a)For safety tell the children to start off slowly and then increase the speed, only making turning jumps when they can see a space.

(b) Remind children to tilt and sway as well as turning and jumping.

[5] Return to your first space in the room, gradually letting the movements die down until you are in your first starting position again. Your magic carpet is about to land. Hold on tightly. Jerk your whole body to show the bumpy landing.

Teaching point

A tense body position and a sudden movement to show the jolt will help.

[6] What can you see? Is it friendly or frightening? Choose a still position to show this.

Teaching point

Facial expressions, focus and posture will contribute to the effect.

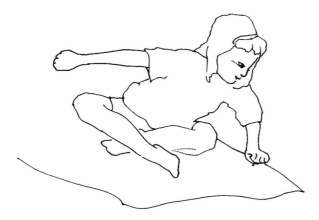

Looking over the edge

Making the dance

Perform all the sections one after the other. Think ahead so that you join together all the parts of the dance smoothly.

Teaching point

Allow the children to decide for themselves when they change from each section. However some may need prompting.

Sharing the work

Half class demonstrations. Observers are asked to look for those dancers who create the impression of flying on the magic carpet.

Possible developments

⟨1⟩ Another section of the dance could be exploring the terrain where they land, e.g. rocky, spongy, cold, deserted.

⟨2⟩ A thunderstorm during the ride.

⟨3⟩ Starting the dance by buying a carpet, unrolling it and discovering it is magic.

6.3 Late For School

The actions of waking, eating breakfast then hurriedly getting to school are the stimuli for this unit, particularly focusing on whole body actions, changes of level and speed.

Resources

Music: 'Dawn chorus'. *Dance Notes.* Brian Madigan (available from Freepost 118, 23 Gloucester Road, Enfield, Middlesex EN2 0BR).

Exploring the ideas

☐1 Sit down and find a curled body shape. Show me how you yawn. Now use your arms and stretch at the same time. Make the yawn even bigger by using your whole body. Now try doing the same actions kneeling but still starting with a curled position. Lastly repeat the actions from high starting position.

Teaching point

Performing the movement at different levels will help to take it from mime into dance.

☐2 Choose whether you are going to roll, fall or spring out of bed. Practise several ways of doing this and remember the one you think is the most unusual.

Teaching point

Encourage children to select their most original idea.

☐3 What do you eat for breakfast? Answer me in movement. Show me whether you are spreading, slicing, scooping, pouring. Now make the action larger again by using your whole body, even your legs.

Teaching points

(a) Children may use only one action or link two or three.

(b) Emphasise the need for precision as they perform their action(s) so that the children know exactly, e.g. the pathways of their gestures.

Yawning

56

4 Suddenly you notice the time. Quickly jump into your school clothes ready to go. Run fast, dodging other people and changing direction quickly as you scurry to school. Jump into your place, sit up straight as fast as you can, ready to work.

Teaching points

(a) SAFETY. Ensure the children can control the speed of their actions.

(b) Dodging high and low as they duck and weave will add to the effect.

Making the dance

Perform your yawning and stretching actions, one sitting, one kneeling, one standing, in any order, followed by your chosen way of getting out of bed. Add the eating breakfast pattern. When the teacher gives a signal, get dressed and race off to school. Finish your dance sitting still in the classroom.

Teaching points

(a) The signal could be spoken, a clap or a bell ringing.

(b) The end position in each section is the beginning of the next. Children may need time to work on these transitions.

Sharing the work

Each child watches another and comments to him or her on whether she or he could see very fast or slow movements. Some are selected by the teacher to be shown to the whole class.

Teaching point

Images such as 'Watching a video in slow motion or on fast forward', will help pupils to understand the contrast.

Possible developments

Any episode representing activities in school, e.g. opening books, writing on the board, playtime.

The teacher's own notes

6.4 Jack and the Beanstalk

This well-known story gives rise to a partner dance between two very different characters.

Resources

1. The story of Jack and the Beanstalk.
2. Pictures of giants.
3. Music: Various tracks from *Peter and the Wolf*. Sergei Prokofiev.

Exploring the dance

1 Jack's adventure. Walk around the room in time with the music swinging your arms and looking about you for something to do. To your surprise you find that the beans that were planted have grown into giant trees. You decide to climb up the tallest one. Stretching your arms and legs one after the other, show how you would pull yourself up the beanstalk with plenty of energy.

Teaching point

The use of focus, e.g. watching where they place their feet, looking upwards as they climb.

2 Jack finds the giant. Practise tiptoeing about. Freeze every time you hear the teacher clap. Can you stop in a shape to show how frightened you are? Keep very still in case the giant sees you.

Teaching points

(a) Moving on hands and feet will add variety to the creeping actions.
(b) Looking up in the still positions will create the impression of hiding from the giant.

3 The giant wakes. Start in a sitting or lying position and wake up using giant sized movements to stretch, yawn and stand up. Stomp around the room with huge steps looking to see what might have woken you. Use your whole body to show you are angry at being disturbed.

Teaching point

Emphasise powerful actions. Making the body wide as well as tall will also enhance the effect.

Jack hiding from the giant

58

Making the dance

Join with a partner and choose which person is Jack and which is the giant. The dance begins with the giant asleep as Jack walks about, and climbs the beanstalk. Jack freezes as the giant wakes up. Now make a partner dance with the giant stomping about and looking around whilst Jack tiptoes and freezes when he thinks he might be discovered. The dance ends with Jack chopping down the beanstalk and the giant slowly tumbling to the floor.

Teaching points

(a) Jack and the giant need to co-ordinate their actions. One method of achieving this is to watch each other throughout.

(b) Offer opportunities for the children to change roles.

Sharing the work

The teacher selects some pairs, who capture the feeling of the two characters, to demonstrate, then the remainder show their dances.

Teaching point

The observers try to notice what makes the dance effective and put this into practice in their own performance.

Possible developments

1. Other sections of the story.
2. More tales about giants.

The teacher's own notes

6.5 Riding my Bike

The theme finishes with a dance performed in groups of fours using the wheeling and pedalling actions of a bicycle.

Resources

1. Pictures of a variety of models of bicycles, e.g. Penny Farthing, tandem.
2. Children's own experiences.
3. Music: 'Legs'. *Art of Noise*. China WOMC 1010.

Exploring the ideas

1 Pedalling. Decide on a member of your four who will be the first leader. Stand in a line behind him/her and copy the way s/he travels in a follow the leader about the room. Leaders, choose your route carefully as though you were steering your bicycle in and out of all the other dancers. Don't forget to give everyone a chance to lead.

Teaching points

(a) Any way of travelling on the feet, e.g. walking, running, jumping or combinations of these can be suggested.

(b) Advise leaders that not changing the action too frequently will help the group to follow.

2 Pumping tyres. Imagine you have a puncture. Everyone show how you would pump up the tyre again. Make the action big and energetic.

Teaching point

Ask the children to perform this in unison with the other members of their four. Using the rhythm of the music will help.

3 Wheeling actions. Working together in your fours, show me how the wheels turn. Can you make circles with your body in different ways?

Teaching points

(a) Children may use gestures, turns or a mixture of these. Using various parts of the body other than the arms will extend the range of ideas.

(b) Ask children to contrast their actions with those of other members of their group.

Pedalling actions

Making the dance

Start your dance travelling (pedalling) as a group. Now stop to pump your tyres and then pedal on to finish with your group wheeling section.

Teaching point

Ensure that each group member has a turn at leading.

Sharing the work

Watch another group. See if they are in time with each other.

Possible developments

Dances about other forms of transport.